KT-438-563

THE STORY OF THE
SHIP

Written by Richard Humble
Illustrated by Peter Cornwall
and Chris Forsey

SIMON & SCHUSTER
YOUNG BOOKS

First published in 1993 by
Simon & Schuster Young Books
Simon & Schuster Limited
Campus 400
Maylands Avenue
Hemel Hempstead
Hertfordshire HP2 7EZ

Planned and produced by
Andromeda Oxford Limited
11-15 The Vineyard
Abingdon
Oxon OX14 3PX

Copyright © Andromeda Oxford Limited 1993

All rights reserved. No part of this publication may be reproduced,
stored in a retrieval system or transmitted in any form or by any
means electronic, mechanical, photocopying, recording or otherwise,
without the permission of the copyright holders.

ISBN 0-7500-1455-5
Printed in Singapore

Foreword

This book tells the story of the oldest form of long-distance transport – the ship. Since the time of the Ancient Egyptians, ships have been carrying men and their goods across the seas and oceans of the world. For most of the 5,000 years since then, men have also built ships of war, designed to win control of the sea in naval battles.

The first ships were simple craft, driven by a single sail and light enough to be rowed as well as sailed. By the late 15th century, bigger ships with more than one mast and roomy cargo-holds were able to cross the world's widest oceans. Ships of that time were also being armed with the latest weapon of land warfare – the cannon. For the next 350 years, sea battles were fought between fleets of wooden sailing ships armed with two or three decks of heavy guns.

About 150 years ago, the ship was transformed. Steam power and the new technology of building with iron and steel had arrived. The new steamships soon brought the age of sail to an end. The story continues into the 20th century with the aircraft carrier, the submarine, and the most luxurious form of travel ever known – the passenger liner.

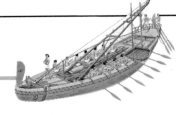

6 Egyptian warship

8 Greek trireme

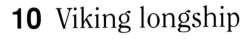

10 Viking longship

12 Ship of war

14 Ship of the line

16 Steamship

18 Clipper ship

Contents

20 Ironclad

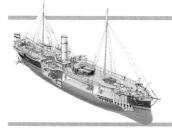

22 Turret ram

24 U–boat

26 Aircraft carrier

28 Ocean liner

30 Glossary

32 Index

Egyptian warship

Below is one of the ships which was sent to attack Syria by Sahure, Pharaoh of Egypt, in about 2400 BC. The Ancient Egyptians were great sailors, and left many pictures showing how they built boats and ships nearly 5,000 years ago.

They were the first people to build open wooden ships with a big square sail to catch the wind, and oars for rowing in harbour and calm weather. Although it was improved greatly over the centuries, the same sort of ship was still being used by the Vikings 3500 years later.

4 The Egyptians used a two-legged mast, which was lowered when the ship was being rowed. When raised, the mast carried a single square sail.

3 The high bow-post of Egypt's warships carried the 'all-seeing eye' – a good-luck charm to bring the ship safely home.

2 A belt of twisted rope was stretched tightly around the hull above the waterline. This helped to keep the planks firmly together. It gave the hull more strength.

1 The narrow bow is a weak point because it takes the full force of the waves. The Egyptians made their boats stronger by tying a tightly twisted rope under the bow from side to side.

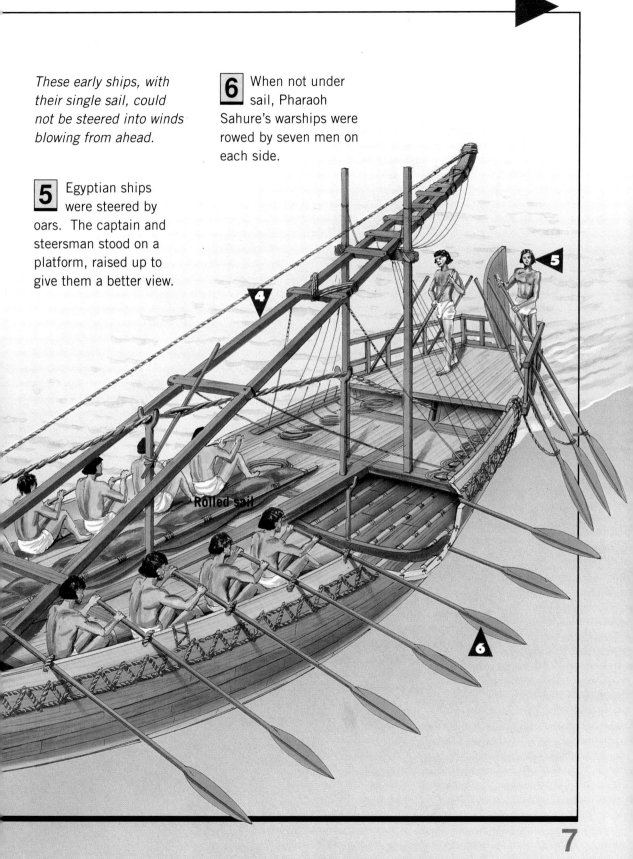

These early ships, with their single sail, could not be steered into winds blowing from ahead.

6 When not under sail, Pharaoh Sahure's warships were rowed by seven men on each side.

5 Egyptian ships were steered by oars. The captain and steersman stood on a platform, raised up to give them a better view.

Rolled sail

Greek trireme

By 500 BC, the Greeks had become the first seafaring people to build a ship designed specially for fighting at sea. This was the trireme, a light, fast war galley which had a pointed ram jutting from its bow. The ship was called a trireme because it had three rows, or banks, of oars. The trireme was used to smash and sink enemy ships in battle.

In 480 BC the Greek trireme fleet saved Greece from conquest by the Persian Empire. It destroyed a powerful Persian fleet in a famous sea battle at Salamis.

The trireme had a special device called an outrigger, stretching out from the ship's side. This enabled such a narrow ship to carry so many oars in more than one bank.

2 The ship was usually steered by twin stern oars. To make a sharp turn, the rowers on one side would stop while those on the other side carried on rowing.

1 The captain (called a 'trierarch') commanded the ship from the stern.

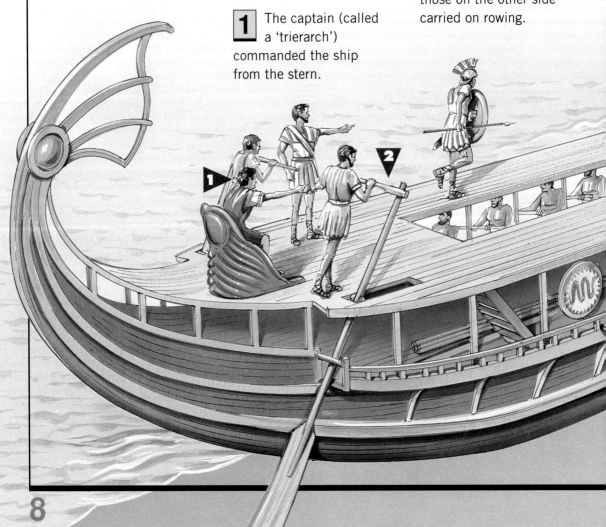

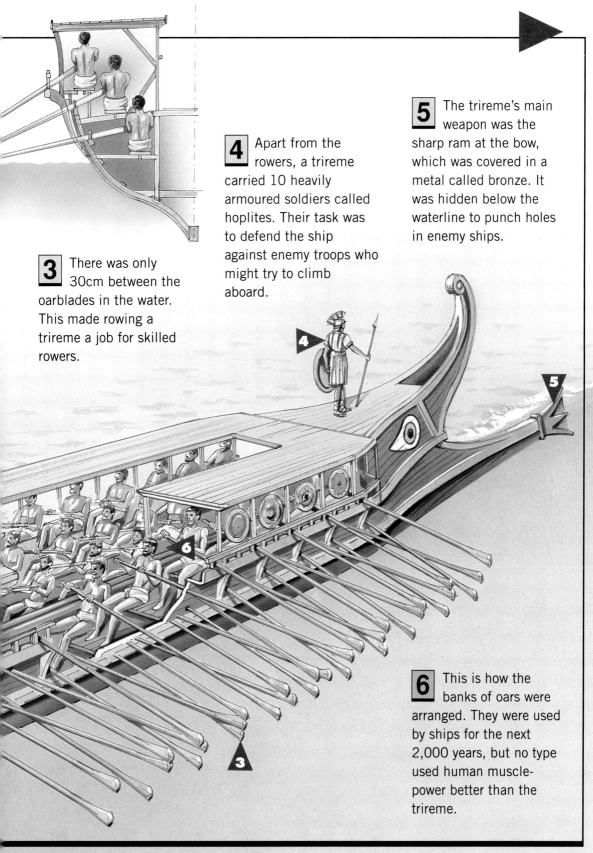

3 There was only 30cm between the oarblades in the water. This made rowing a trireme a job for skilled rowers.

4 Apart from the rowers, a trireme carried 10 heavily armoured soldiers called hoplites. Their task was to defend the ship against enemy troops who might try to climb aboard.

5 The trireme's main weapon was the sharp ram at the bow, which was covered in a metal called bronze. It was hidden below the waterline to punch holes in enemy ships.

6 This is how the banks of oars were arranged. They were used by ships for the next 2,000 years, but no type used human muscle-power better than the trireme.

Viking longship

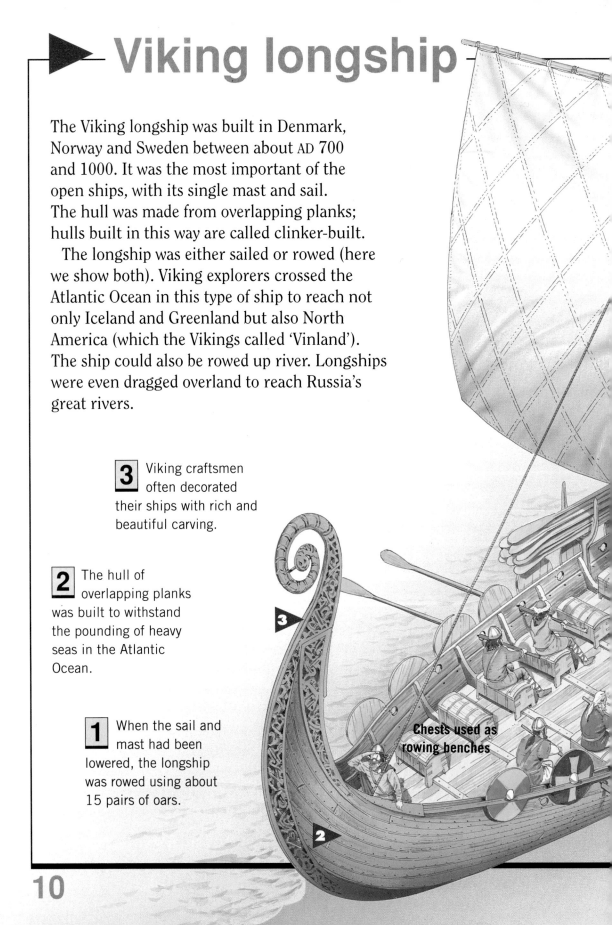

The Viking longship was built in Denmark, Norway and Sweden between about AD 700 and 1000. It was the most important of the open ships, with its single mast and sail. The hull was made from overlapping planks; hulls built in this way are called clinker-built.

The longship was either sailed or rowed (here we show both). Viking explorers crossed the Atlantic Ocean in this type of ship to reach not only Iceland and Greenland but also North America (which the Vikings called 'Vinland'). The ship could also be rowed up river. Longships were even dragged overland to reach Russia's great rivers.

3 Viking craftsmen often decorated their ships with rich and beautiful carving.

2 The hull of overlapping planks was built to withstand the pounding of heavy seas in the Atlantic Ocean.

1 When the sail and mast had been lowered, the longship was rowed using about 15 pairs of oars.

Chests used as rowing benches

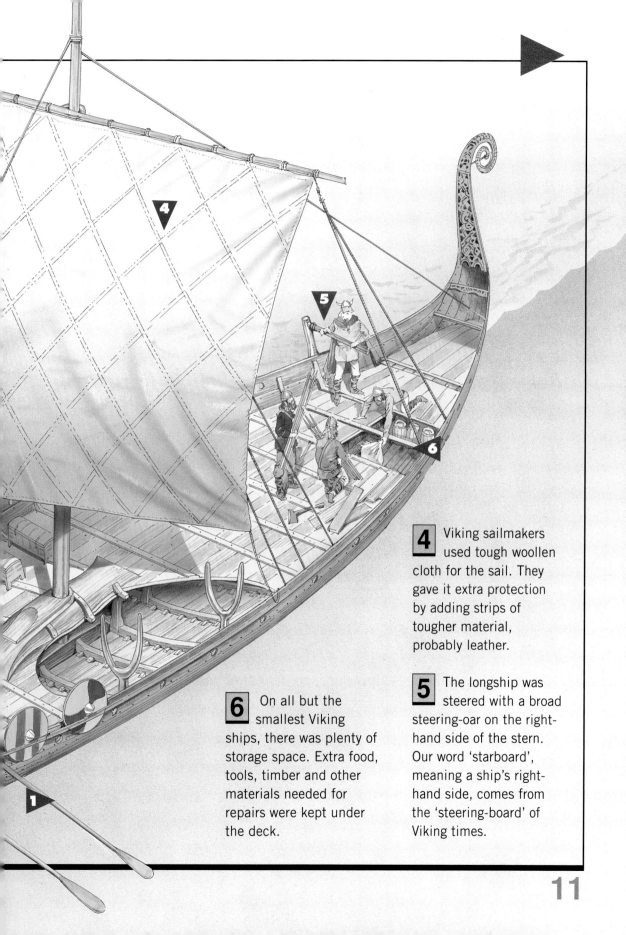

4 Viking sailmakers used tough woollen cloth for the sail. They gave it extra protection by adding strips of tougher material, probably leather.

5 The longship was steered with a broad steering-oar on the right-hand side of the stern. Our word 'starboard', meaning a ship's right-hand side, comes from the 'steering-board' of Viking times.

6 On all but the smallest Viking ships, there was plenty of storage space. Extra food, tools, timber and other materials needed for repairs were kept under the deck.

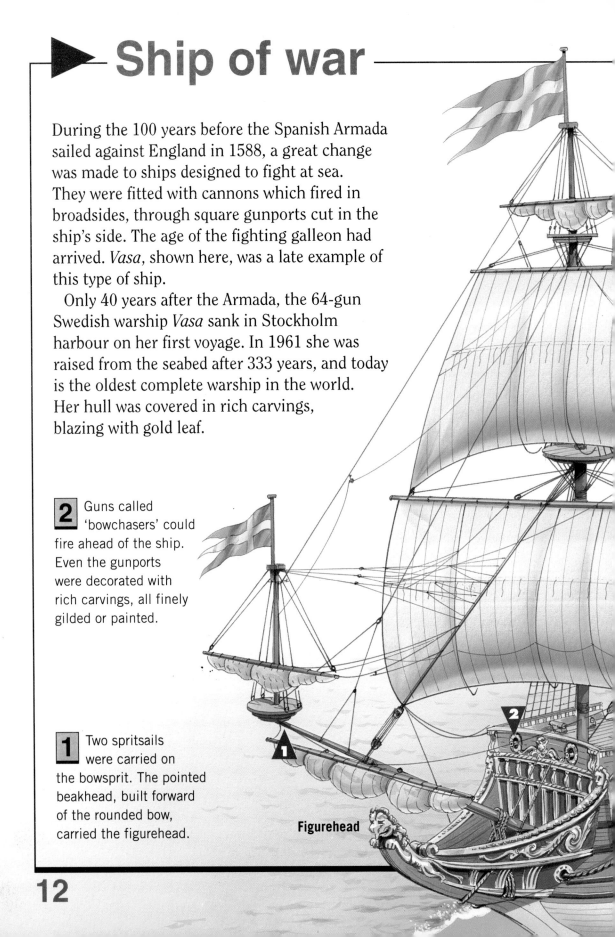

Ship of war

During the 100 years before the Spanish Armada sailed against England in 1588, a great change was made to ships designed to fight at sea. They were fitted with cannons which fired in broadsides, through square gunports cut in the ship's side. The age of the fighting galleon had arrived. *Vasa*, shown here, was a late example of this type of ship.

Only 40 years after the Armada, the 64-gun Swedish warship *Vasa* sank in Stockholm harbour on her first voyage. In 1961 she was raised from the seabed after 333 years, and today is the oldest complete warship in the world. Her hull was covered in rich carvings, blazing with gold leaf.

2 Guns called 'bowchasers' could fire ahead of the ship. Even the gunports were decorated with rich carvings, all finely gilded or painted.

1 Two spritsails were carried on the bowsprit. The pointed beakhead, built forward of the rounded bow, carried the figurehead.

Figurehead

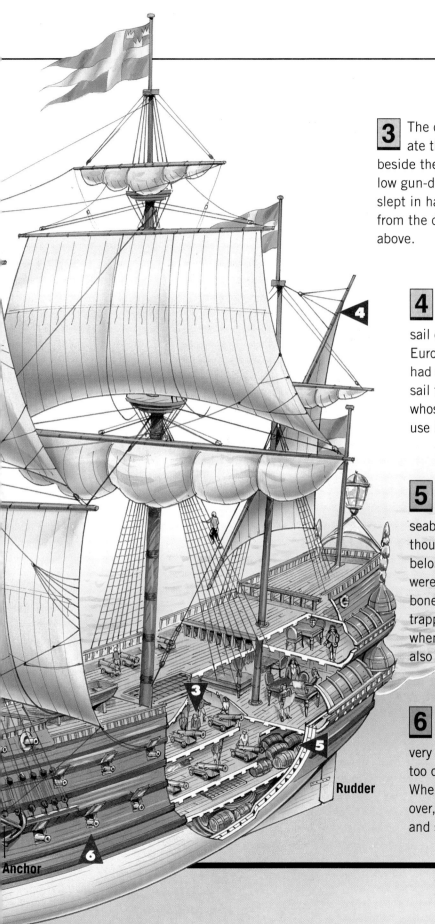

3 The crew lived and ate their meals beside their guns on the low gun-decks. They slept in hammocks slung from the deckbeams above.

4 *Vasa* carried a triangular 'lateen' sail on her mizzenmast. European ship designers had copied this type of sail from the Arabs, whose sailing dhows still use it today.

5 When *Vasa* was raised from the seabed in 1961, thousands of items belonging to the crew were found inside. The bones of 18 people trapped below decks when *Vasa* sank were also found.

6 The lowest row of gunports in *Vasa's* very slim hull was much too close to the water. When the ship heeled over, the water flooded in and sank her.

Rudder

Anchor

Ship of the line

Built 130 years after *Vasa*, Britain's HMS *Victory* is the last surviving 'ship of the line'. These were battleships carrying two or more decks of heavy guns, which formed the 'line of battle'. They were used in great sea fights like Trafalgar (21 October 1805).

These powerful warships were divided into groups, or 'rates', depending on how many guns they had. *Victory* was a 'first rate', which meant she had 100 guns or more. 'Second rates' had between 84 and 100 guns, and 'third rates' between 70 and 84. *Victory* was launched in 1765. She was crewed by 850 officers and men.

3 The crew's hammocks were stowed in netting which ran around the deck, giving extra protection from enemy fire.

2 The heaviest of *Victory*'s 104 guns were the two huge 'smashers' on the foredeck. They fired 30.8kg balls.

1 Building the *Victory* used up 8,490 cubic metres of timber – a forest of oaks which had taken 100 years to grow.

4 If the steering wheels were shot away in battle, the ship was steered by men hauling on the rudder tiller below decks.

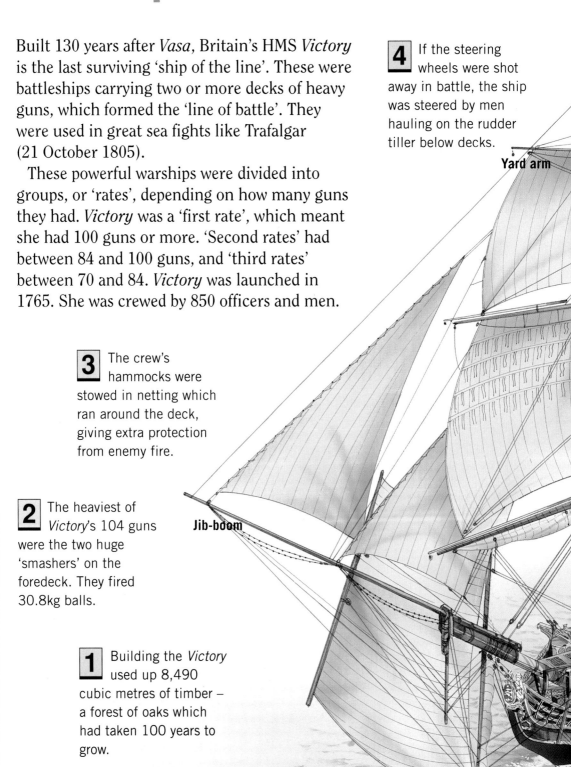

Yard arm

Jib-boom

Foremast

Mainmast

Mizzenmast

5 In battle, wounded men were carried below to the ship's lowest deck, below the waterline and out of reach of enemy fire.

6 There were three gun-decks and 102 guns.

Steamship

Few other ships have ever achieved so many 'firsts' as *Great Britain*, built in 1843. She was the first large ship (3,676 tonnes) to be built wholly of iron; the first to be driven by a propeller instead of by side paddlewheels; the first to use watertight compartments as a safety measure; and the first to be given bilge keels.

Great Britain made her first Atlantic crossing in 1845, and was in use for nearly 40 years. She could carry both passengers and cargo.

1 *Great Britain*'s screw propeller was very advanced for its time. Instead of the simple two-bladed screw carried by most steamships, *Great Britain*'s was six-bladed.

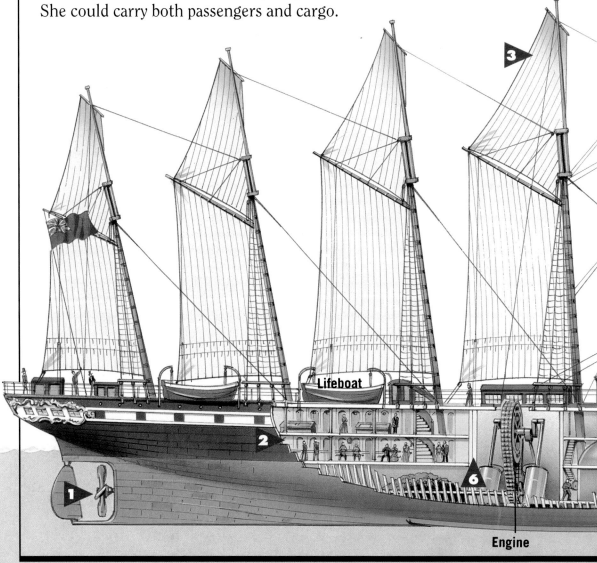

Lifeboat

Engine

2 *Great Britain* was also the first modern passenger liner. She had staterooms (luxury cabins) for 60 passengers who travelled in first-class comfort.

3 Like all other early steamships, *Great Britain* did not rely on her engines. She could also carry 1,393sq.m of sail on six masts.

4 To improve her performance in high seas, *Great Britain* had a very sharp bow.

5 Bilge keels made the ship roll less in rough weather and made sailing more comfortable.

6 The roomy hull was divided into six compartments by watertight bulkheads as a safety precaution.

Boiler

Clipper ship

'Clippers' were so called because they were the fastest sailing ships in the world and were able to clip days off the sailing-time of any other ship. They were built to transport passengers and cargoes over long distances in the shortest possible time.

Clippers carried American emigrants to California around Cape Horn; Australian wool to Britain; and tea from China to London. The record London to Australia voyage was 60 days. Clippers were widely used between 1850 and 1870. Even then, however, they could not travel as fast, or carry such big cargoes, as the new steamships.

3 On all three masts, small extra sails could be added. These were called 'studding-sails'.

2 Named from the bottom upwards, the basic types of sails on all three masts were called the courses, the topsails, the top-gallants and the royals.

1 Built for extra strength, the overhanging counterstern helped protect this part of the ship from waves.

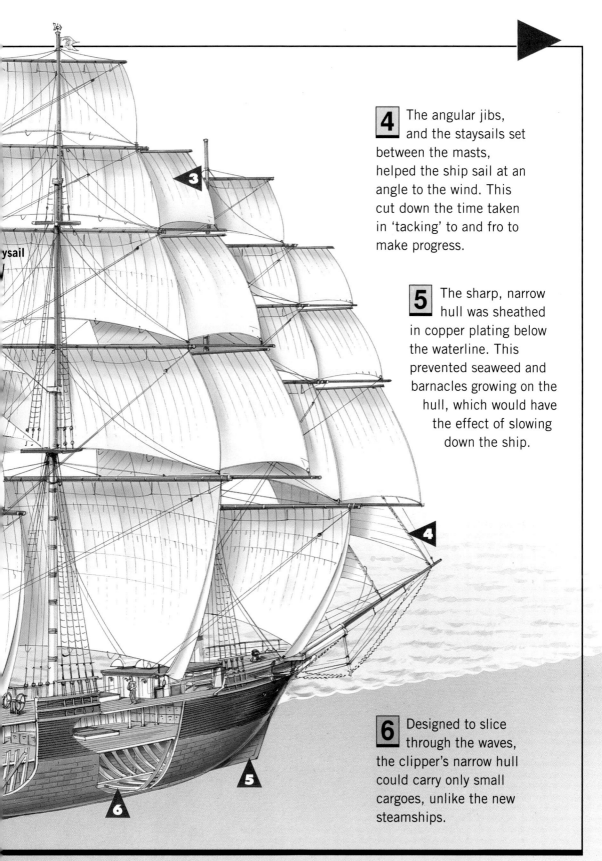

4 The angular jibs, and the staysails set between the masts, helped the ship sail at an angle to the wind. This cut down the time taken in 'tacking' to and fro to make progress.

5 The sharp, narrow hull was sheathed in copper plating below the waterline. This prevented seaweed and barnacles growing on the hull, which would have the effect of slowing down the ship.

6 Designed to slice through the waves, the clipper's narrow hull could carry only small cargoes, unlike the new steamships.

ysail

Ironclad

By the 1850s, wooden warships were proving to be no match against modern guns firing explosive shells instead of solid shot. The only protection against shellfire was metal armour plate. The 'ironclad' warship had arrived.

Warrior, today restored and on public display at Portsmouth, England, was the first of these new 'ironclads' built for the British Navy. She was launched in 1860 and was designed both to sail and to use steampower. She had a broadside of 17 guns a side and an armoured 'belt' 11.4cm thick.

3 *Warrior*'s two funnels were raised only when the engines were used. They were lowered when the ship ran on sails alone.

2 *Warrior* carried a full rig of masts and sails. This freed her from having to stay near ports where stocks of coal for her engine could be easily obtained.

1 The gun battery was covered by armour plating, but the rest of the ship had only iron plates. These were too thin to protect against a bursting shell.

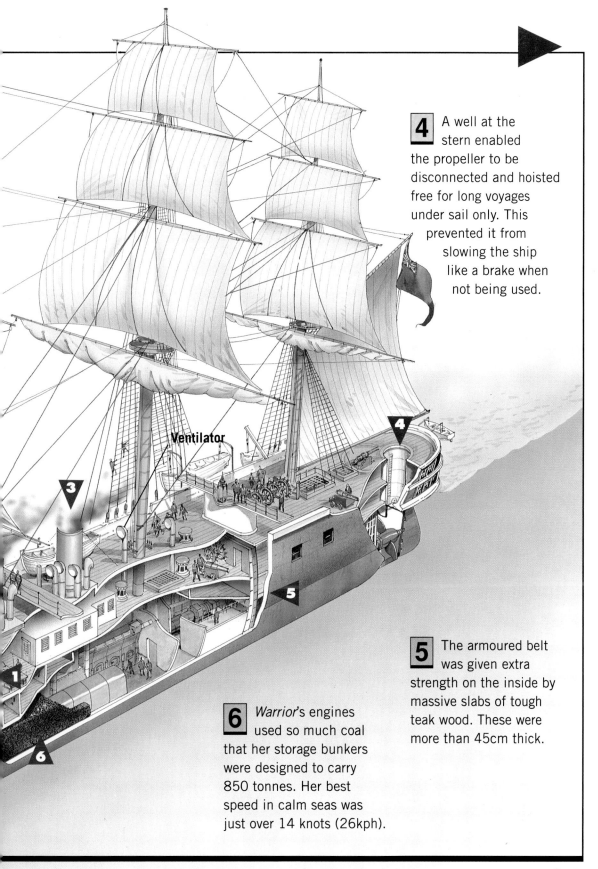

4 A well at the stern enabled the propeller to be disconnected and hoisted free for long voyages under sail only. This prevented it from slowing the ship like a brake when not being used.

Ventilator

5 The armoured belt was given extra strength on the inside by massive slabs of tough teak wood. These were more than 45cm thick.

6 *Warrior*'s engines used so much coal that her storage bunkers were designed to carry 850 tonnes. Her best speed in calm seas was just over 14 knots (26kph).

Turret ram

Launched in 1868, only seven years after *Warrior*, the ironclad ship *Buffel* (the name means 'Buffalo') was built in Britain for the Dutch Navy. *Buffel* was one of the world's first warships to be driven by steam only. She also carried two heavy guns in a rotating turret.

For nearly 300 years, warships had fought with their guns, not by ramming enemy ships as ancient oared galleys had done. By the 1860s, however, steam-engined ships with steel hulls made ramming attacks possible again, and *Buffel* had a strengthened bow for ramming. But she never saw battle, and today she is a museum ship at Rotterdam, Netherlands.

3 The two sailors manning the ship's steering wheel at the aft of the ship were completely exposed to the weather and enemy fire. Steering the ship would have been very uncomfortable in bad weather.

2 *Buffel* was one of the first warships in the world to be driven by twin propellers. Both propellers were driven by a separate engine. She could travel at over 12 knots (22.2kph) in a calm sea. This was extremely fast for the late 1860s.

1 Below decks there was plenty of living space for the crew, and separate cabins for the officers. *Buffel* was later used as a floating barracks for Dutch Navy sailors.

4 *Buffel* was commanded from a light, open bridge running from side to side across the centre of the ship. This gave an excellent all-round view, but had no protection against bad weather or enemy fire.

5 The circular turret contained two heavy guns firing shells 22.9cm wide. The turret could turn around to fire on the enemy.

6 *Buffel*'s main weapon, after her guns, was the armoured ram-bow, jutting forward below the waterline. It was designed both to withstand enemy shells and to survive the tremendous shock of a ramming attack.

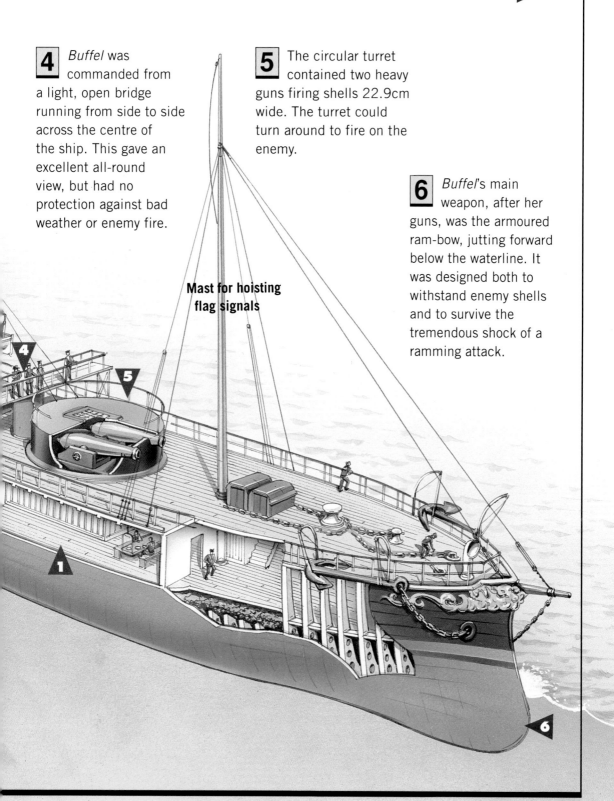

Mast for hoisting flag signals

U-boat

The submarine shown here is a Type VII German U-boat or 'undersea boat' of the Second World War (1939–1945). Like all submarines, it dived by flooding tanks on the side of the hull with seawater, and surfaced by blowing the tanks empty with compressed air. Its main weapon was the torpedo. After it was fired, the torpedo ran below the surface and burst against the hull of the target ship.

The first successful submarines used petrol engines on the surface and an electric motor running on batteries when submerged. Later submarines used diesel engines which were more powerful.

2 Powerful diesel engines drove the U-boat at 16 knots (29kph). This was much faster than most other small warships.

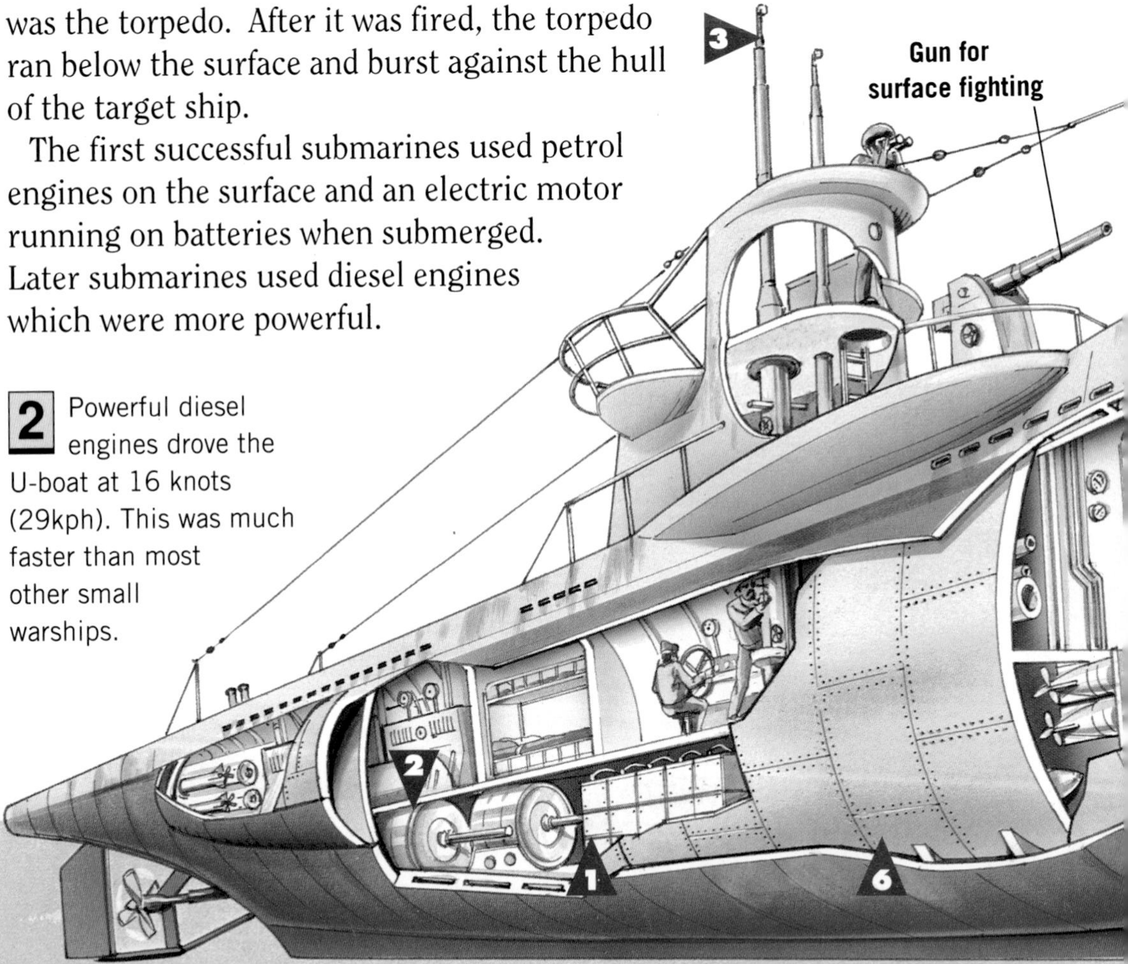

3 When lying just below the surface, the U-boat captain raised the periscope to look for targets. The periscope was lowered when the U-boat dived.

Gun for surface fighting

1 The batteries for the electric motor were recharged by the diesel engines each time the U-boat surfaced.

6 The ballast tanks, open to the sea for easy filling and emptying, surrounded the inner hull where the crew lived.

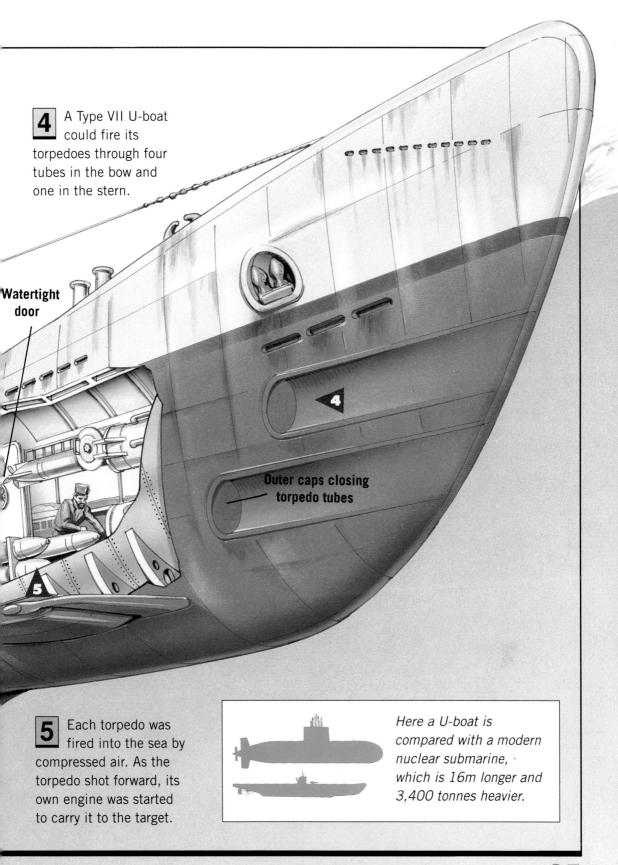

4 A Type VII U-boat could fire its torpedoes through four tubes in the bow and one in the stern.

Watertight door

◀ 4

Outer caps closing torpedo tubes

5

5 Each torpedo was fired into the sea by compressed air. As the torpedo shot forward, its own engine was started to carry it to the target.

Here a U-boat is compared with a modern nuclear submarine, which is 16m longer and 3,400 tonnes heavier.

Aircraft carrier

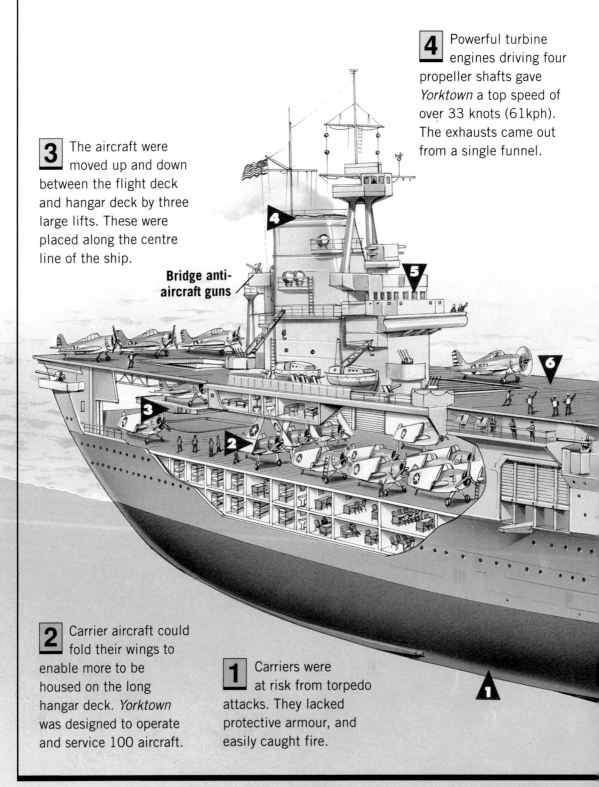

4 Powerful turbine engines driving four propeller shafts gave *Yorktown* a top speed of over 33 knots (61kph). The exhausts came out from a single funnel.

3 The aircraft were moved up and down between the flight deck and hangar deck by three large lifts. These were placed along the centre line of the ship.

Bridge anti-aircraft guns

2 Carrier aircraft could fold their wings to enable more to be housed on the long hangar deck. *Yorktown* was designed to operate and service 100 aircraft.

1 Carriers were at risk from torpedo attacks. They lacked protective armour, and easily caught fire.

5 Called the 'island', the carrier's bridge and funnel structure was placed on the starboard side of the ship.

6 To launch and recover aircraft, the carrier had to steam at full speed into the wind. Catapults, powered by compressed steam, were used to launch the heaviest types of aircraft.

The aircraft carrier was developed during the final years of the First World War (1914–1918). It gave fleets the power to launch air attacks on enemy ships far from land airfields, while defending themselves from enemy air attack. In the Second World War (1939–1945) rival fleets with aircraft carriers fought air battles without the ships of either fleet ever sighting each other.

An aircraft carrier is a floating air base. It has large stocks of aircraft fuel and weapons, a hangar deck to which aircraft can be lowered for repairs, and an upper flight-deck where the aircraft take off and land. Shown here is the famous American carrier *Yorktown*, completed in 1937.

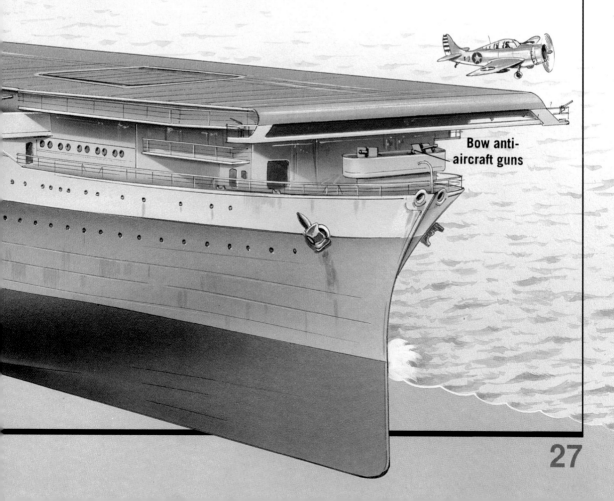

Bow anti-aircraft guns

Ocean liner

Developed at the end of the last century, the passenger liner was the most luxurious form of travel ever known. The most important route was across the Atlantic between the United States and Europe. The world's greatest liners competed for the 'Blue Riband of the Atlantic', awarded for the fastest crossing.

Because aircraft can travel so fast, ocean liners have become less important for this type of travel. But ocean liners are still used for luxury holidays at sea.

3 Since the luxury liner *Titanic* sank with the loss of 1,589 lives in 1912, all passenger liners must carry enough lifeboats and emergency rafts to hold everyone who goes to sea in them.

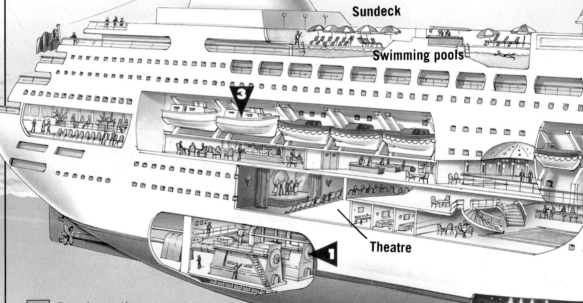

Sundeck

Swimming pools

Theatre

Discotheque

2 Rough weather causes the ship to pitch from bow to stern, and roll from side to side. Modern cruise liners are fitted with wing-like stabilisers to help reduce these movements.

1 The engines are designed to be very quiet, smooth and economical. Luxury liners no longer need high-speed engine power.

4 Modern ships have better aids to safe navigation than at any time in history. These include radar (to avoid collisions) and electronic navigation systems using special orbiting satellites out in space.

5 A modern cruise liner is specially designed to give passengers every possible enjoyment. It has luxury restaurants, lounges, playrooms for children, a cinema, indoor and outdoor sports, and at least one swimming pool.

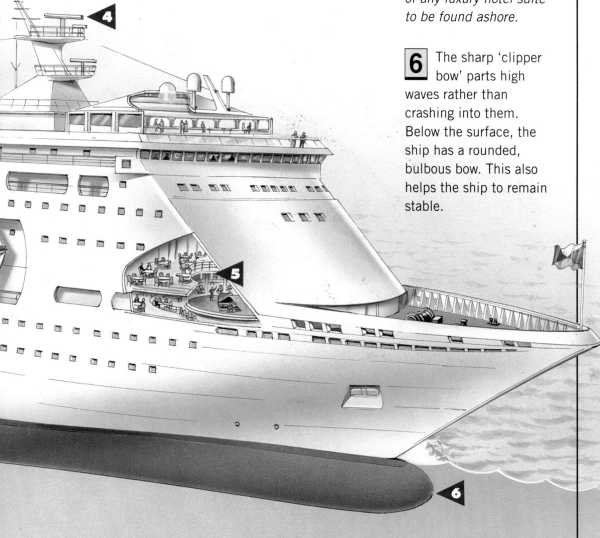

A deluxe cabin, offering passengers the facilities of any luxury hotel suite to be found ashore.

6 The sharp 'clipper bow' parts high waves rather than crashing into them. Below the surface, the ship has a rounded, bulbous bow. This also helps the ship to remain stable.

Glossary

Aft
Towards the stern in a ship.

Ballast tanks
Tanks which are flooded to make a submarine dive, and are pumped full of air to make it surface.

Beakhead
Pointed structure built out from a sailing ship's bow.

Bilge keels
Long narrow plates on the underside of a ship, on either side of the central keel.

Bow
The pointed front end of a ship.

Bow post
The strong timber rising from the front of a wooden ship's keel.

Bowchaser
A gun placed to fire straight ahead of the ship.

Bowsprit
Large spar mounted in a sailing ship's bow, from which spritsails or jibs are set (attached).

Bridge
Raised platform on the deck of a ship, from which the ship is commanded.

Broadside
All the guns on one side of a ship, arranged to fire together.

Bulkhead
A wall between compartments and cabins inside a ship.

Counterstern
A ship's stern which is high and curved, instead of square.

Courses
The largest square sails of a ship set on the lowest yards.

Deck beam
The beams running from side to side in a ship, supporting the decks.

Dhow
A type of Arab sailing ship with lateen sails.

Figurehead
Ornamental carved figure, mounted on the beakhead of a sailing ship.

Fore
Towards the bow of a ship.

Forecastle
The living quarters of a ship's crew, beneath the foredeck.

Foredeck
The forward deck of a ship, often raised above the level of the upper deck.

Galley
A ship's kitchen. Also a light, narrow warship driven by oars.

Gunport
Square hole cut in a ship's side for a gun to fire through.

Headwind
A wind blowing on to the bow of a ship, making progress difficult.

Hull
The main body of a ship, supporting masts and rigging.

Island
The bridge structure of an aircraft carrier, placed to the side of the flight deck.

Jibs
Small triangular sails, set between a ship's foremast and bowsprit.

Keel
The lowest timber or line of plates in a ship, from which the hull is built up.

Kites
Small extra sails set to get the most speed from the wind in fine weather.

Lateen sail
A large triangular sail, running fore and aft, carried on a long slanting yard.

Line of battle
The line formed by a fleet's heaviest ships when preparing for battle.

Moonrakers
Small extra sails, set in fine weather.

Periscope
A long tube with viewing glasses, for seeing above the surface from a submarine under water.

Propeller
The rotating screw which drives an engine-powered ship forward.

Ram
A pointed projection for damaging the hull of enemy ships.

Royals
The sails set above the top-gallants.

Rudder
The hinged timber or metal plate hung at the stern, for changing the ship's direction.

Ship of the line
A sailing battleship with two or more gun-decks, powerful enough to join the line of battle.

Skysails
The sails set above the royals.

Spritsails
The sail or sails set below the bowsprit.

Staysails
Triangular sails set between the masts.

Stern
A ship's rear end.

Studding-sails
Small extra sails set on either side of the yards in fine weather.

Tacking
Steering a zig-zag course to make progress against a headwind.

Top-gallants
The sails set above the topsails.

Topsails
The sails set above the courses.

Torpedo
A missile fired to sink an enemy ship by exploding beneath the waterline.

Trireme
A Greek war galley rowed by three levels or banks of oars.

Waterline
A line on a ship's hull marking where the water will reach.

Yards
Strong poles hung from the masts, from which the sails are set (attached).

Index

aircraft 26–27, 28
  carrier 26–27
all-seeing eye 6
American emigrant 18
anchor 12
Arab 13
Atlantic 16, 28
Australian wool 18

beakhead, pointed 12
bilge keel 16, 17
boiler 17
bow 6, 17, 22, 23, 25, 28, 29
bowsprit 12
bridge 23, 27
bronze 9
Buffel 22–23
bulkhead, watertight 17

captain 7
cargo 16, 18, 19
carving 10, 12
catapult 27
clinker-built ship 10
clipper ship 18–19
coal 20–21
compressed air 24

deck 11, 14, 22
  hangar 26–27
  upper flight 26–27
Denmark 10
dhow 13

Egyptians, Ancient 6
electric motor 24
enemy fire 14, 15, 22, 23
  ships 8–9, 22
engine 16, 28
  diesel 24
  petrol 24

figurehead 12
foredeck 14
foremast 14
funnel 20, 27

galleon 12
galley 8, 22

Great Britain 16–17
Greek 13
gun 22, 23
  anti-aircraft 26, 27
  battery 20
  heavy 14
  modern 20
gun-deck 13, 15
gunport 12, 13, 15

hammock 13, 14
hull 6, 10, 12, 24
  copper plated 19
  slim 13
  steel 22

iron plate 20

jib 19
  boom 14

lifeboat 28
long-distance ship 18
longship 10–11

mainmast 15
mast 19, 20
  single 10
  two-legged 6
metal armour 20
mizzenmast 13, 15

oar 6, 7, 8, 10
  bank 8
  steering 11
  stern 8
open ship 10
outrigger 8

paddlewheel 16
passenger 16, 18, 29
  liner 28–29
periscope 24
Persian Empire 8
Pharaoh Sahure 6–7
propeller 16, 21, 22
  screw 16

radar 29

ram 8, 9, 23
rower 8–9
rowing bench 10
rudder 13
rudder tiller 14

sail 6–7, 10, 12, 13, 17, 18,
  20–21
  woollen 11
stabiliser 28
starboard 11
steamship 17, 18, 19, 20–21,
  22–23
steering wheel 14, 22
steersman 7
stern 8, 25, 28
  counter- 18
storage space 11
submarine 24–25
  nuclear 25
Sweden 10

tank
  ballast 24
  flooding 24
timber 10, 11, 14
Titanic 28
torpedo 24–25, 26
trierarch 8
trireme 8–9
turret, rotating 22–23

U-boat 24-25

Vasa 12–13, 14
ventilator 21
Victory 14–15
Viking 6, 10–11

Warrior 20–21, 22
warship 7, 8, 20–21, 22–23
  Egyptian 6
  oldest 12
  rate 14

waterline 6, 9, 15, 19

yard arm 14
Yorktown 26-27